MW00584070

IN HONOR OF LOWER WALNUT STREET BUSINESSES
AND PEOPLE WHO MADE BRONZEVILLE HAPPEN.

Green Bay Fish Market-Polansky
Bach's Deli
Brookstaff Economy Store-Rachall
818 W. Walnut St.
Tompkins Ice Cream Parlor:
Johnnie V. Caldwell
816 W. Walnut St.
Silverstein Grocery Store
Mason, N.A. Tailor Shop
732 W Walnut St.
West Indian Herb Products Co:
Rev. Chief J. Ruffino
916 W. Walnut St.
Regal Theatre: Sid Market
704 W. Walnut St.
Hillside V&V Market
Hillside Home Appliance Merchandise
612 W. Walnut St.
W.A Mason Co. Tailor Shop
732 W. Walnut St.
Matherson's Haberdashery
623 W. Walnut St.
Handsome Barber Shop: R.C Moore
828 W. Walnut St.
Reasby's Garage & Body Shop
328 W. Walnut St.
Apex Amusements-Livery Service (Cabs)
819 W. Walnut St.
Advertising (Radio): Mannie Mauldin Jr.
612 W. Walnut St.
Harlem Record & Appliance Shop
919 W. Walnut St.
NAACP: W. Dale Phillips (president)
702 A.W. Walnut St.
Attorney's: Coggs, Theodore
635 A. W. Walnut St.
Dorsey, James W.
635 W. Walnut St
Phillips, Dale
707 A.W. Walnut St.
Phillips, Mrs. Vel
707 A. W. Walnut St.
Blaskovics Inc- Live & Dresses Poultry
1101 W. Walnut St.
Colonial Barber Shop
610 W. Walnut St.
Deluxe Barber Shop
939 W. Walnut St.
Veterans Barber Shop
1017 W. Walnut St.
Blanche's Beauty Chest
726 W. Walnut St.
Deluxe Beauty Clinic
838 W. Walnut St.
Sally's Beauty Shop
1116 W. Walnut St.
Vogue Beauty Salon
923 W. Walnut St.
Josey J. Anthony-Bookkeeper
729 W. Walnut St
Carpenters & Contractors: Barron, James
907 W. Walnut St
Robert Finney
606 W. Walnut St.
Decon Jones Chicken Shack
537 W Walnut St.
Larry's Chicken Shack
619 W. Walnut St.
Lloyd's Drug Store
725 W. Walnut St.
Boatner's Chili
709 W. Walnut St.
Dr. Kenneth L. McIver
1202 W. Walnut St.
Greater Galilee Baptist Church:
Rev. M.J. Battle (pastor)
808 W. Walnut St.
St. Matthew C.M.E. Church:
Rev. W.J.G. McLin (pastor)
Band Box Cleaners
839 W. Walnut St.

Tal & Griff's Valet Services
909 W. Walnut St.
Rev. G.W. McDuffy
710 B. W. Walnut St.
Rev, Chief J. Ruffino
916 W. Walnut St.
Rev. William Rush
508 W. Walnut St.
Rev. Maridy L. Andrews
Sidney's Furniture
1129 W. Walnut St.
Fort Nite Club: Mrs. Frank McIntyre
905 W. Walnut St.
Bentley's Clothing & Jewelry
1138 W. Walnut St.
Tastee Freez
717 W. Walnut St.
700 Tap: Bob Brown
700 W. Walnut St.
711 Taverns : Jo Harris & Willie Morris
711 W. Walnut St.
Kokomos: Bonnie Qualls
Cleo's Flowers
535 W. Walnut St.
Pembroke Coal & Ice Co.
612 W. Walnut St.
O'Bee Funeral Home: Emile O'Bee Sr.
617 W. Walnut St.
Jones Service Station
603 W. Walnut St.
Tanker Gas Station
735 W. Walnut St.
Josey J. Anthony- Income Tax Consultant
729 W. Walnut St.
Insurance Salesman Underwriter:
Leroy Simmons
1204 W. Walnut St.
Mrs. Cleo Reed- Insurance Salesman
535 W. Walnut St.
T. Joe's Self Service Launderette:
T. Joe & Ruth Thomas
718 W. Walnut St.
King Solomon-Lodge of Ancient York Mason:
Walter Taylor (grand master)
811 W. Walnut St.
James C. Jackson- 20th Century Cleaners &
Dryers Inc
332 W. Walnut St.
Mrs. Hivell Gibbs c/o Lloyd's Drugstore
(pharmacists)
725 W. Walnut St.
Physicians: Dr. Henry A. Fletcher
720 W. Walnut St.
Dr. William R. Rose
833 W. Walnut St.
Dr. Cyril F. Turney
508 W. Walnut St.
Pastine Poole Hall
1035 W. Walnut St.
725 Pool Hall
725 W Walnut St.
Johnson Agency Real Estate Agencies
921 W. Walnut St.
Clara's Restaurant
722 W. Walnut St.
Jon & Luo's Steak House
835 W. Walnut St.
Knox Music Café
608 W. Walnut St.
Lousiana Fine Food
322 W. Walnut St.
Gold Coast Bar
638 W. Walnut St.
Riley Cook Upholstering
635 W. Walnut St.
Dr. A. R. Wiener (dentist)
Big Milt Super Bar: Milton Brill
1039 W. Walnut St.
The Bop Shop: Shorty Moore
612 W. Walnut St.

Submitted by Normajean C. Sims (BillieJo)
Historian of the Walnut Street Social Gathering

Bronzeville - A Milwaukee Lifestyle

IN HONOR OF LOWER WALNUT STREET BUSINESSES AND PEOPLE WHO MADE BRONZEVILLE HAPPEN.

Green Bay Fish Market-Polansky
Bach's Deli
Brookstaff Economy Store-Rachall
818 W. Walnut St.
Tompkins Ice Cream Parlor:
Johnnie V. Caldwell
816 W. Walnut St.
Silverstein Grocery Store
Mason, N.A. Tailor Shop
732 W Walnut St.
West Indian Herb Products Co:
Rev. Chief J. Ruffino
916 W. Walnut St.
Regal Theatre: Sid Market
704 W. Walnut St.
Hillside V&V Market
Hillside Home Appliance Merchandise
612 W. Walnut St.
W.A Mason Co. Tailor Shop
732 W. Walnut St.
Matherson's Haberdashery
623 W. Walnut St.
Handsome Barber Shop: R.C Moore
828 W. Walnut St.
Reasby's Garage & Body Shop
328 W. Walnut St.
Apex Amusements-Livery Service (Cabs)
819 W. Walnut St.
Advertising (Radio): Mannie Mauldin Jr.
612 W. Walnut St.
Harlem Record & Appliance Shop
919 W. Walnut St.
NAACP: W. Dale Phillips (president)
702 A.W. Walnut St.
Attorney's: Coggs, Theodore
635 A. W. Walnut St.
Dorsey, James W.
635 W. Walnut St
Phillips, Dale
707 A.W. Walnut St.
Phillips, Mrs. Vel
707 A. W. Walnut St.
Blaskovics Inc- Live & Dresses Poultry
1101 W. Walnut St.
Colonial Barber Shop
610 W. Walnut St.
Deluxe Barber Shop
939 W. Walnut St.
Veterans Barber Shop
1017 W. Walnut St.
Blanche's Beauty Chest
726 W. Walnut St.
Deluxe Beauty Clinic
838 W. Walnut St.
Sally's Beauty Shop
1116 W. Walnut St.
Vogue Beauty Salon
923 W. Walnut St.
Josey J. Anthony-Bookkeeper
729 W. Walnut St
Carpenters & Contractors: Barron, James
907 W. Walnut St
Robert Finney
606 W. Walnut St.
Decon Jones Chicken Shack
537 W Walnut St.
Larry's Chicken Shack
619 W. Walnut St.
Lloyd's Drug Store
725 W. Walnut St.
Boatner's Chili
709 W. Walnut St.
Dr. Kenneth L. McIver
1202 W. Walnut St.
Greater Galilee Baptist Church:
Rev. M.J. Battle (pastor)
808 W. Walnut St.
St. Matthew C.M.E. Church:
Rev. W.J.G. McLin (pastor)
Band Box Cleaners
839 W. Walnut St.

Tal & Griff's Valet Services
909 W. Walnut St.
Rev. G.W. McDuffy
710 B. W. Walnut St.
Rev, Chief J. Ruffino
916 W. Walnut St.
Rev. William Rush
508 W. Walnut St.
Rev. Maridy L. Andrews
Sidney's Furniture
1129 W. Walnut St.
Fort Nite Club: Mrs. Frank McIntyre
905 W. Walnut St.
Bentley's Clothing & Jewelry
1138 W. Walnut St.
Tastee Freez
717 W. Walnut St.
700 Tap: Bob Brown
700 W. Walnut St.
711 Taverns : Jo Harris & Willie Morris
711 W. Walnut St.
Kokomos: Bonnie Qualls
Cleo's Flowers
535 W. Walnut St.
Pembroke Coal & Ice Co.
612 W. Walnut St.
O'Bee Funeral Home: Emile O'Bee Sr.
617 W. Walnut St.
Jones Service Station
603 W. Walnut St.
Tanker Gas Station
735 W. Walnut St.
Josey J. Anthony- Income Tax Consultant
729 W. Walnut St.
Insurance Salesman Underwriter:
Leroy Simmons
1204 W. Walnut St.
Mrs. Cleo Reed- Insurance Salesman
535 W. Walnut St.
T. Joe's Self Service Launderette:
T. Joe & Ruth Thomas
718 W. Walnut St.
King Solomon-Lodge of Ancient York Mason:
Walter Taylor (grand master)
811 W. Walnut St.
James C. Jackson- 20th Century Cleaners &
Dryers Inc
332 W. Walnut St.
Mrs. Hivell Gibbs c/o Lloyd's Drugstore
(pharmacists)
725 W. Walnut St.
Physicians: Dr. Henry A. Fletcher
720 W. Walnut St.
Dr. William R. Rose
833 W. Walnut St.
Dr. Cyril F. Turney
508 W. Walnut St.
Pastine Poole Hall
1035 W. Walnut St.
725 Pool Hall
725 W Walnut St.
Johnson Agency Real Estate Agencies
921 W. Walnut St.
Clara's Restaurant
722 W. Walnut St.
Jon & Luo's Steak House
835 W. Walnut St.
Knox Music Café
608 W. Walnut St.
Lousiana Fine Food
322 W. Walnut St.
Gold Coast Bar
638 W. Walnut St.
Riley Cook Upholstering
635 W. Walnut St.
Dr. A. R. Wiener (dentist)
Big Milt Super Bar: Milton Brill
1039 W. Walnut St.
The Bop Shop: Shorty Moore
612 W. Walnut St.

Submitted by Normajean C. Sims (BillieJo)
Historian of the Walnut Street Social Gathering

C.L. Johnson
Founder of the Booker T. Washington Y.M.C.A.
Courtesy of Irene Goggans

BRONZEVILLE
A Milwaukee Lifestyle

by
Ivory Abena Black
Cultural Anthropologist

Preface by Dr. Reuben Harpole

Edited by Sally Di Frances

Volume 1

THE PUBLISHERS GROUP

This work is dedicated to the ancestors and descendents of Milwaukee's Bronzeville.

The Publishers Group

Copyright 2005 Revised 2006 by The Publishers Group, LLC
ISBN 0-9771065-0-0

Published by The Publishers Group
Ivory Abena Black, Faithe Colas, Patricia Diggs, Publishers
Washington DC, Los Angeles, CA,
Milwaukee, Wisconsin, Ghana West Africa

Printed in Port Washington, Wisconsin Port Publications

Graphic Design Clark Graphics, Milwaukee, Wisconsin

For all general information and orders contact
The Publishers Group
www.bronzeville-milwaukee.com
E-mail sales@bronzeville-milwaukee.com

This book by no means depicts the entire history of Bronzeville Milwaukee. This is an introduction and overview.

About the Book Cover photograph:
First Group of Black Youth who went to YMCA Camp Minikani in 1945.

Cover Photo Courtesy of Irene Goggans

Table of Contents

Acknowledgements to those who made this book possible.

Attorney Leonard V. Brady, Irene Goggans, Dr. Reuben Harpole, Jerrel W. Jones, Anita Johnson, Brad Pruitt, Dr. Mary Ellen Shadd Gaines, Normajean Sims, Gina Thomas, Anthony Tatum, Marcus Mays, Urban Anthropology Inc. and Attorney Nola Cross

TO ALL THOSE WHO ARE PROUD OF MILWAUKEE'S AFRICAN AMERICAN HISTORY, HERITAGE AND CULTURE.

Rod and Gun Club, Annual Wild Game Dinner
December 28, 1950

Courtesy of Irene Higgins

Welcome To
Bronzeville - A Milwaukee Lifestyle

Larry's Lunch-ette

619 West Walnut Street   COncord 4-9713

"WHERE CHICKEN IS KING and FROZEN CUSTARD QUEEN"

WHEN IN THE MOOD FOR FINE FOOD

Specializing in Southern Fried Chicken

Hot Plate Lunches and Jumbo Hamburgers

Orders Prepared to Take Out

LAWRENCE HILL, Prop.

Larry's Lunchette. Bronzeville was host to many Black-owned restaurants.
Negro Business Directory 1951-1952. Courtesy of Irene Goggans

The Right Spot Tap. There were numerous Black-owned venues with impeccable customer service.
Negro Business Directory 1951-1952. Courtesy of Irene Goggans

THE RIGHT SPOT TAP

BEER — LIQUOR — FOOD

"Service on the Dot"

1239 N. 6th St.   Alex Bassett, Prop.   BRoadway 2-8443

preface

This is the second book that has been written specifically about Black Milwaukee. I am overjoyed that the publisher's have taken this project on. The Northwest Ordinance of 1787 prohibited slavery in the new territories. This provision was upheld when Wisconsin became a "free state" in 1848. African Americans have been a part of Wisconsin since the very beginning. Joe Oliver, the cook for one of the three founders of Milwaukee, voted in Milwaukee's first election. Cecil Arm's family participated in the Civil War's Wisconsin regiments, eighty-five thousand troops volunteered to fight, and twelve thousand lost their lives, Black and White. In addition there are many towns and streams that are named after African Americans in Wisconsin.

My hat goes off to Faithe Colas, Ivory Abena Black and Patricia Diggs for undertaking the task of writing about the rich history of Blacks in Milwaukee. This effort is a start. I would like to acknowledge that there is so much more that can be written about Black Milwaukee.

There is the history of the athletes, scholars, social civic clubs, the blue collar workers, the professionals, the churches, the businesses, the teachers, Prince Hall Masonic, Eastern Stars, the Chatter Box Club, The Esquister's Club, Ten Gentlemen's Clubs, The Clarence Johnson Y Rod and Gun Club, Lake Ivanhoe, Milwaukee Pan Hellenic Council, Eta Phi Beta, Zeta Phi Beta, The Milwaukee Young Professionals, The Urban League, The N.A.A.C.P. and The Metropolitan Milwaukee Alliance of Black School Educators. The fine arts of our community are really second to none in the United States. I hope that you enjoy reading about this great community and its people.

Dr. Reuben Harpole - Historian, Milwaukee, Wisconsin

LOcust 2-5663   Hours: 8 A. M. to 7 P. M.

Cleo's Flower Shop
Artistic Arrangements
Flowers for All Occasions
MRS. CLEO REED, Proprietor

535 W. Walnut St.   Milwaukee, Wis.

Cleo's Flower Shop
Artistic Arrangements
Flowers for All Occasions
MRS. CLEO REED, Proprietor

forward

Journeys, stories and moments of time. This book is in part the fulfillment of my journey back home to Milwaukee. I left Milwaukee 25 years ago on my life journey, spending 10 years in Los Angeles and 15 years in Washington D.C. in media and communications. In 2003, while managing a mayoral campaign for the first African American mayor of Alexandria Virginia, I received a call from my Aunt in Mississippi, to come home because my father had suffered a severe stroke. My world stopped like a stopwatch and I began my journey back home.

My parents came to Milwaukee in 1955 from a segregated and hostile South searching for a better life, as did most African Americans in Milwaukee. My father worked 35 years at Ladish Co. as a machinist and my mother 25 years for Milwaukee County. They created a stable family life sending my siblings and myself to a private high school and college. In the 1990's, my parents sold their house in Milwaukee, retired and built a house in Mississippi. The severity of my fathers' stroke brought him to a nursing home in Milwaukee. Here is where I started to hear the stories from the nursing home residents about a community that was built on style and pride, Bronzeville – Milwaukee. My father passed away that summer leaving me with a "whisper" to tell the stories of Bronzeville-Milwaukee to the world.

My search for Bronzeville-Milwaukee began on a walking tour with Ivory Abena Black a cultural anthropologist. She is a walking National Geographic full of the knowledge and history of African Americans in Milwaukee. We developed a creative publishing team with Faithe Colas, publisher of the Milwaukee Courier and began our sacred journey to tell the stories of our parents and proudly place them on the shelves of Milwaukee history.

I thank those who have supported me: Dr. Howard Fuller, Fred Gordon, Martha Love, my darling Aunt Mae Covington, cousin Hazel Thaddison, Dana Pearl, Janice Malone, Sylvia Scott (LA Law), Dr. Michelle Ferrier, Carol Porter, Bob Asher and all my friends at the Washington Post. I dedicate this forward to the loving memory of my parents Watson Diggs Jr. and Mary L. Diggs and the "alley cats of 16th street": Mr. Washington. Mr. Meyers, Mr. Jones and Mr. Kern. A champagne toast to the Cadillac cars, Stetson hats and Stacy Adams shoes.

Welcome to Bronzeville-Milwaukee.

Patricia A. Diggs - Publisher, Bronzeville A Milwaukee Lifestyle

Beautiful.... Bronze....   People....... of Milwaukee,

we

have traveled a great distance through

history and time sculpting and engineering the world's humanity....... We find

ourselves in Milwaukee now.

Gifted in all areas of science, we erected

massive empires and monuments that can be found in Ethiopia, Egypt, and

Spain....... We are here in Milwaukee now.

Our divine schools of thought were in

Salamanca, Spain and the University of Sankore in Timbuktu, which was the

world's first educational Mecca in the Western Sudan. We come from a great

and mighty people who chose to remain standing progressing forward.

We are now here in

Milwaukee and hold a great knowledge that can be found all through out the

city's history and culture......

We.... are.....

here....

_____Ivory Abena Black_____

4

For as long as I can remember, I have always been enthusiastic about world history and culture. It started when I was a young girl and my mother, Irene Black, bought me a set of National Geographic books for Christmas. I would page through the magazine amazed at all of the different places and people the earth housed. For the first time I saw people of many worlds so different from my own. It was not until my junior year in college that I became aware of Milwaukee's rich African American culture. I took an internship with Urban Anthropology, Inc., and discovered that the organization conducted research on different cultural groups in Milwaukee, including African Americans. I asked myself, "Why had no one told me that African Americans had a history in Milwaukee?" It was then that I learned about the unique heritage of African Americans in Milwaukee and the creation and lifestyle of the Bronzeville community. This new found enlightenment literally propelled me to search for Milwaukee's African American history.

During my journey, I met Reuben Harpole, one of Milwaukee's leading African American historians. He told me that C.L. Johnson and Bernice Lindsay were the father and mother of the African American community. Beechie Brooks, president of United Realty Group gave me a clear insight into the origin of Halyard Park. Halyard Park was created from years of hard work, patience, and lots of saving of the old mighty dollar. Pictures really do tell a story and when I met Clayborn Benson, founder of the Wisconsin Black Historical Society Museum, he showed me the faces of African Americans in Milwaukee dating all the way back to the 1800's. I could not believe my eyes. I saw pictures confirming our existence and history in Milwaukee. My journey has been long and is not yet complete. For the pursuit of Milwaukee's African American history has been silently waiting for the right souls to come along to tell the story. Here, in Milwaukee we have a fascinating history well documented by our achievements all the way back to our first migration into the city. It is important to note that if the youth of our communities are not well versed on this wealth of historical knowledge, history is bound to repeat itself. African Americans in this city have a rich heritage full of true pioneers who overcame hardship and worked together for progress. Their triumphs need to be remembered and passed on to our children now and for generations to come.

Ivory Abena Black

~

COLUMBIA SAVINGS AND LOAN ASSOCIATION

1924   26 Years   1951

Of Home Financing and Thrift Promotion. Fifty consecutive dividends paid indicates outstanding record of dividend payment.

Current Rate 3%

Accounts Insured up to $5,000 by an Agency of the Federal Government

Wilbur Halyard, Secretary-Treas.

2236 North 8th Street

The Columbia Savings and Loan Association was established September 26, 1924 by Wilbur and Ardie (Clark) Halyard. The banking association provided loans to sustain the growth of the Black community.
Negro Business Directory 1951-1952.
Courtesy of Irene Goggans.

High Wide and Handsome Club. Bronzeville was host to many social and civic clubs that provided comradeship and fun.
Negro Business Directory 1951-1952. Courtesy of Irene Goggans

High Wide and Handsome Club

Slogan—Aim at the moon and shoot at the stars.
The president Carl Crowley resides at 613-A West Vine Street
LOcust 2-3135

chapter one

HISTORICAL OVERVIEW

African Americans first entered Wisconsin's history as tradesmen with French fur traders in the 1700's. As an abolitionist state with a high density of industrial type jobs, Wisconsin attracted many African Americans seeking education, financial stability, and refuge from the tormenting South. Escaped slaves commonly traveled the Mississippi River which was part of the Underground Railroad, as a guide to freedom. Many African Americans went to safe havens in Canada, Illinois, Michigan, and Ohio, but some would stay in Wisconsin to live their lives as freed men and women. Two notable cases involving runaway slaves and the Underground Railroad occurred in Milwaukee. The history of runaway slaves, Caroline Quarrels and Joshua Glover, is thought to be the best documented. Yet many African Americans seeking freedom in Milwaukee are known, but the history and documentation of their struggles is fragmented.

Only 16 years of age, Caroline Quarrels, could not withstand one more day of callous bondage. In 1843 she left St. Louis, Missouri by steamboat, becoming a fugitive American slave. The first stop towards freedom was in Alton, Illinois, where she passed as a White school child. Shortly after, an African American man seeing she was not White assisted her to a stagecoach headed for Milwaukee, Wisconsin (1). It did not take long for the identity of this daring woman to be discovered. A former friend tried to betray her for $300, but she was quickly informed of this deception and went back on the run. Asahel Finch, one of Milwaukee's leading attorneys at the time, aided the young woman to a hiding place where she would be safe. From there a team of abolitionists fought to keep Caroline Quarrels hidden from slave hunters all the way to her final destination in Windsor, Canada (2).

In 1852, Joshua Glover, with the help of the Underground Railroad, escaped from a plantation in Missouri, seeking freedom and social justice. He went to Racine, Wisconsin and worked in a saw mill. As the story goes, on March 4, 1854, Joshua Glover was playing cards with some friends in his cabin. In the mix of laughter and gambling, a loud bang rattled the cabin door. Glover being on alert, quickly advised his friend not to open the door without asking who was there. It was too late. His friend unlocked the door and in came a U.S. Marshal, five armed men, and Joshua Glover's former slave master, Benjamin S. Garland. Garland was armed with a pistol (3). The men beat Glover until he was no longer able to respond and took him to Cathedral Square Park where Milwaukee's first courthouse jail was

THELMA'S BACK DOOR

"Where Your Cares Steal Silently Away"

Mixed Drinks A Specialty—Television and Nightly Entertainment

701 West Juneau Avenue   BRoadway 2-2760

Thelma's Back Door. Many Bronzeville venues were located in downtown Milwaukee.
Negro Business Directory 1951-1952. Courtesy of Irene Goggans.

located. Sherman M. Booth, editor of the abolitionist newspaper, *The American Freeman*, began to organize a public meeting that afternoon. After the meeting a mob of abolitionists attacked the jail with pick axes to free Glover. They rushed him back to Racine, Wisconsin, and then onto a steamship to Canada.

Booth was arrested for "aiding and abetting" Joshua Glover's escape on March 15, 1854 (4). He was eventually pardoned by President Buchanan in 1861, but lost his newspaper worth a fortune of $60,000.

Not all African Americans who arrived to make a living in Wisconsin came as fugitive slaves. Charles Edward Shepard, the first African American resident of Grant County, founded Pleasant Ridge in 1849. Paying only $1.50 per acre, he and his family were able to acquire land. During the Fugitive Slave Act of 1850, they helped many runaway slaves find refuge. Near Lancaster was Green Colony, a once thriving African American settlement founded by Lester Green (5). Green was a porter on a commuter train that traveled daily between Wisconsin and Illinois. He is said to have died a millionaire after investing in the stock market. It did not take long for African Americans to make their presence known in Milwaukee. In 1835, after sailing the Great Lakes as a cook on the schooner Cincinnati, Joe Oliver, Milwaukee's first reportedly known African American man, came ashore to work for Solomon Juneau, Milwaukee's first mayor. Joe Oliver was more than a cook. In the year of his arrival, he marked history by casting the first ballot as an African American, in Milwaukee's first election on September 17, 1835(6). He would return to the schooner after 1837 and sail for some time on the C.C Tow Bridge. He died in 1842 from small pox. His spirit lives on as Milwaukee's first African American founding father.

Thus far, the first known African American family, the Watsons, came to Milwaukee in 1850. Patriarch, Sully Watson, a whitewasher, would acquire a lot on East Mason Street where his family resided. From there the Watson family would expand, eventually allowing their son, William Thomas and his wife Julia to build their home on the lot. Just a block away on 3rd and Sycamore Streets, now Michigan Avenue, was Sully's elder daughter, Ann Georgina Anderson (6). The African American family and community would become more prominent as a steady influx of African Americans arrived in Milwaukee.

At the beginning of the century only ten percent of African Americans lived above the Mason Dixon line and most worked as tenant farmers or sharecroppers in the South. After the passing Civil War, many ventured towards the industrial North and traveled to places like New York, Philadelphia, and Chicago, where they established small communities (7). Of course they came to Milwaukee as well.

9

Most worked as skilled laborers, factory hands, or small businessmen but the majority as waiters, house servants, or unskilled laborers. African Americans held strong work and family ethics, and eventually were lead to great success in Milwaukee.

Milwaukee's African American population would increase gradually, consisting of 14 barbers, 7 cooks, 6 whitewashers, 3 masons, and 1 farmer in a community of 100 people by the late 1800's. By the late 1920's to early 1930's, African Americans in Milwaukee had settled in one square mile area bound by West Brown, West Juneau, North Third and North 12th Streets. Three-fourths, 78.2%, of Milwaukee's African American population were reported by the 1940 census to be living in this area consisting of 74 blocks. Half, 52.8%, of the 13,059 population were reported by the census to be of African descent (8). Due to hardening racial tension, African Americans were faced with social and economic restraints that kept them confined to areas generally bordered by State Street to North Avenue, and between Third to 12th Streets on Walnut. This area would soon be known as Bronzeville.

Walnut Street Business District 1950's
Courtesy of Milwaukee Public Library

chapter two

BRONZEVILLE
A Community of Family and Spirit

The largest migration of African Americans into Milwaukee took place between 1905 and 1935. During this time African Americans poured into the city to be employed, primarily in domestic and personal service positions. With the European population dominating industrial occupations, African Americans found themselves working as servants and cooks to White clientele. The coming of World War II would change the lifestyle for Milwaukee's African American working class as the number of European immigrants declined due to conflict and war. This shortage in White labor would soon make way for African Americans in the city to ascend to middle class status by way of Milwaukee industrialists who had to fill vacant positions in order to sustain their businesses.

Despite the lack of White labor, only 12 of more than 2,000 manufacturing plants hired African American workers. Companies such as the Plankinton Packing, Albert Trostel and Sons Company, The Pfister and Vogel Leather Company, Allis and Chalmers Manufacturing Company, the Falk Company, Milwaukee Coke and Gas Company employed nearly 75% of all African Americans in the industrial field. Others included such companies as the Illinois Steel, A. J. Lindemann and Hoverson Company, National Malleable Iron, Solvay Steel, and B. Hoffmann Manufacturing (9).

Essentially, a higher income would allow African Americans to begin seeking better living arrangements but due to outbreaks of racial tension, African Americans in Milwaukee, especially those newly migrated, found themselves confined to one residential district. Bound by North Avenue Street on the North, State Street on the South, Third Street on the East, and 12th Street on the West, African Americans seeking work would fill and over populate Bronzeville.

The phrase *Bronzeville* was a generic term given to an area in a city in which the majority was populated by African Americans and people of African descent. However, Milwaukee's Bronzeville was not solely occupied by newcomers from the South. Germans, Jews, Italians, and other Eastern Europeans had made their homes there long before the influx of African Americans into the city and were widely interspersed throughout the community. In the late 1800's to early 1900's previous immigrant groups slowly began to move northward, leaving a densely populated African American community immersed in family traditions.

Milwaukee's Bronzeville was a community devoted to close nuclear and extended families. Home to lower, middle and upper classes, African Americans offered guidance to all who lived there that would further the community's progress and relationships. This laid the foundation for a reliable society in which people assisted each other in child rearing, job placement, tutoring, money lending, repair services, medical assistance, and social interactions (10). A city within a city full of leadership, a sense of community, and a focus on entrepreneurship would lead to a high number of African American owned businesses and entertainment venues. Two inspiring individuals who came to Milwaukee should be recognized and honored for presenting this city with its first African American financial institution, Wilbur and Ardie (Clark) Halyard were a truly vital resource for African Americans in Milwaukee. In 1923, residing in Beloit, Wisconsin, the Halyards were shocked by the deplorable housing available to African Americans in Milwaukee (11). The Halyards lived a middle class lifestyle and they knew what it took to gain and maintain that status. They were committed to empowering other African American families to reach the same status through home and business ownership. Aside from racial segregation the Halyards noted that the major dilemma in the African American community was the lack of capital to improve or develop real estate. The Halyards immediately began organizing a savings and loan association to ease the lack of capital by selling bonds to friends and associates. By April, 1923, the ground work to open Milwaukee's first African American savings and loan office would be in process. With strong and steadfast vision, the Halyards would undergo 19 months of training for qualification, supervised by the Wisconsin Department of Banking. Out of this intensive training, the Columbia Savings and Loan Association was born on September 26, 1924. By April 4, 1925, Columbia Savings and Loan Associations would find a home at 486 Eighth Street, providing visibility and status for the African American community (12). The African American community would continue to grow, but only internally. Now, with the means of acquiring a loan through Columbia Savings and Loan Association, middle class African Americans could take their rightful place as leaders in Bronzeville.

A Page of Respect

C.L. JOHNSON FOUNDER OF THE BOOKER T. WASHINGTON Y.M.C.A MILWAUKEE, WISCONSIN

BERNICE COPELAND-LINDSAY FOUNDER OF HILLSIDE TERRACE MILWAUKEE, WISCONSIN

MOTHER AND FATHER OF THE AFRICAN AMERICAN COMMUNITY

As African Americans struggled to find a foothold in the work place, they created strong institutions that cultivated a sense of solidarity. The oldest and strongest of these is the Black church. The first and most thriving church was St. Mark African Methodist Episcopal Church located on Fourth and Kilbourn. By 1915, three major African American churches would emerge, including Calvary Baptist Church and Morris Temple Church of God.

One of the most active leaders at St. Mark African Methodist Episcopal Church was C.L. Johnson, who owned a successful tailoring business and was founder of the Booker T. Washington YMCA on Eighth and Walnut. Johnson became known as the Father of the Black Community. His counterpart, Bernice Copeland-Lindsay, an equally powerful activist who founded the Hillside Terrace was known as the Mother of the Black Community. Lindsay was the first African American director of a Milwaukee YWCA, a position she lost after protesting the YWCA's discriminatory housing practices. These two active pioneers also laid the foundation for a steadfast tradition that helped the community in the administration of job placement, tutoring, repair services, medical assistance, and youth focused organizations.

Bronzeville

chapter three

LOWER WALNUT STREET
THE HEART OF BRONZEVILLE

From Third to roughly Twelfth Streets on Walnut, Milwaukee experienced the birth of numerous African American businesses. Known best as Lower Walnut Street, it became the heart of the community for Bronzeville's lower, middle and upper class residents. The city would soon see a burst of African American culture come to life on Lower Walnut Street where hotels, night clubs, restaurants, barber shops, cafés, frozen custard joints, and chicken shacks emerged as new sources for entertainment and social interaction.

This area of Milwaukee became a vibrant African American social and cultural district, filled with restaurants and clubs where the sounds of Rhythm and Blues were performed live by world's masters, Duke Ellington, Louis Armstrong, and Billie Holiday (13).

Dr. Reuben Harpole, a historical leader in today's Milwaukee African American community, remembers well when famous African American artists would come to Milwaukee to "get down and boogie." Due to segregation and Jim Crow, artists could not stay in Milwaukee downtown hotels. Instead, they stayed right in the community with the residents. Can you imagine having your favorite artist staying in your home? This kind of hospitality gave Bronzeville's residents a real sense of security and trust. Lower Walnut Street in the early 1930's and 1940's was living proof of the strong entrepreneurial spirit of African Americans in Milwaukee.

What made Lower Walnut Street so special was that it was more than just a busy shop-lined street, it was actually the reason why Bronzeville was able to thrive. African Americans and other clientele kept monetary resources within the community's boundaries. This allowed money to circulate from one African American establishment to the next making it possible for everyone to make a decent living. In the mid-1950's to early 1960's two major actions, Urban Renewal and the construction of I-43, would disturpt the community and bring the prosperity of Bronzeville to a halt.

Walnut Street Business District (circa1950's)
Courtesy of Milwaukee Public Library.

CLARA'S RESTAURANT

Clara's Restaurant.
A long standing (29 years) and successful business establishment.
Negro Business Directory 1951-1952. Courtesy of Irene Goggans.

KEEPING BRONZEVILLE ALIVE

Historian Normajean Billie Jo Sims speaks on the Walnut Street Social Gathering Club

Walnut Street Social Gathering Club is a non-profit, non-political, non-sectarian social club that was organized in the late summer of 1988. The idea of this gathering club is to socialize and come together with plans to celebrate life rather than meeting by chance at the memorial service of a departed mutual friend. This club is comprised of senior citizens, who are former residents of Bronzeville.

Walnut Street meetings are held the second Saturday of each month at the Dr. Martin Luther King Jr. Center, located at 1531 West Vliet Street. Original members were Katie Carter Carroll, Dorothy Bailey Dale, Marian (Pat) (Bandy-Barter) Graham, Otha Grider, Clorine Henderson Harris, Thurman Hawkins, Norris Jackson Sr., Carrie Benson Oldham, Gerald Payne, Reverend Clifford Pitts, Normajean BillieJo and Andrew Sims and Earl Williams. Most of the social club's members are retired. Some were city and county employees, educators, police officers, firemen, tavern owners, railroad, postal and factory workers, hotel, hospital and sanitation employees, engineers, truck drivers, and state representatives, doctors, nurses, lawyers, beauticians, barbers and ministers. In the fall of 1989, Walnut Street Social Gathering Club meetings were relocated with the help of member Earl Williams (now deceased). Earl asked Brother Booker Ashe, (also deceased) then director of the House of Peace to allow us to meet there. Bronzeville was home to Black businesses consisting of restaurants, a movie theater, the Regal (not owned by Blacks), barber and beauty shops, churches, YMCA plus local pool halls and taverns. This is part of our history. Our purpose is to keep these memories alive and pass them on.

Membership consists of one hundred and fifty people. Most of the members were born and raised in Milwaukee and attended school at Fourth Street and Ninth Street Grade Schools, Brown Street School, Seifert Grade School, Roosevelt Junior High School, Lincoln, North Division High School, and St. Benedict the Moor School. Some of the members have left Milwaukee and moved to other states, but they return each year on the third Saturday in August to attend the annual cook out which is held in Carver Park, area # 1, at North Ninth and West Brown Streets.

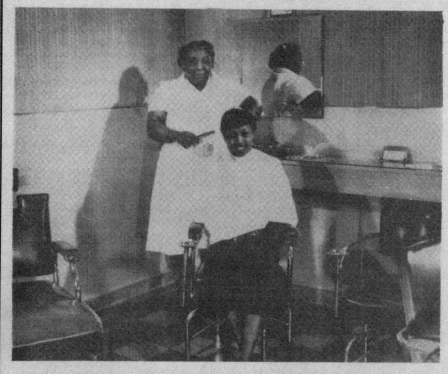

ROSA LEE'S BEAUTY SALON

Mrs. Rosalie Hale, Prop.

*"Distinctive Service in All Lines of Beauty Culture Is Offered You at
Rosa Lee's Modern Well-Ventilated Shop*

So Conveniently Located at 2245 North 6th Street
COncord 4-9620

**Rosa Lee's Beauty Salon, 1951 The talk of the town.
A long standing (29 years) and successful business establishment.**
Negro Business Directory 1951-1952.

LEE'S BEAUTY SAL

chapter four

Urban Renewal & I-43
Wipe out Bronzeville

African Americans living in Milwaukee have seen great success, productivity and change since the arrival of Joe Oliver in 1835. They came to Milwaukee seeking jobs and the city had just what they needed. The dream of being free, self sufficient, and educated was now a reality in the hearts and minds of many African Americans. Bronzeville, with its entrepreneurial spirit was a thriving place for African Americans. However, housing and buildings found on Lower Walnut Street and within Bronzeville were deemed by Milwaukee's power structure to be a slum district.

With the Housing Act of 1949, Congress established the Slum Clearance and Community Development and Redevelopment program. This Act commissioned federal funds to assist cities in eliminating their slums and blighted areas and to provide the maximum opportunity for the redevelopment of project areas by private enterprise. Five years later, Congress further expanded and changed the emphasis of the urban improvement program with the Housing Act of 1954 (14). One of the primary objectives motioned in the Housing Act of 1949 was to provide "a decent home and a suitable living environment for every American family". The government supplied aid to cities in clearing slums and finding private developers for new housing.

The Housing Act of 1954, on the other hand, sought to accomplish the same goal by subsidizing not only new housing but also public improvements that would improve a neighborhood environment (15). With these new requirements, the program came to be known as Urban Renewal, enacted in 1949. To mark the change, the Slum Clearance and Community Development and Redevelopment program was renamed the Urban Renewal Administration. Following a national improvement of America's cities, implemented by the federal government, the city of Milwaukee, in 1950, began developing plans to rid Milwaukee of it's slum area. Administered by Mayor Frank Zeidler, the Urban Renewal Act left many homes and buildings across Milwaukee cleared for revitalization. This also meant removing buildings on Lower Walnut Street and in areas of the African American community, leaving an imprint of blight and civil unrest in the heart of the African American metropolis. At the same time the city was also planning to build the North-South freeway, I-43, which cut directly across Bronzeville, eliminating

19

Homes in Bronzeville 1930's. After the migration of the Germans and Jews to other neighborhoods these houses were left for the new arrival of African Americans to Milwaukee.
Courtesy of Milwaukee Public Library.

over 8,000 homes (16). The rationale for these actions; the city of Milwaukee wanted a way for citizens from areas like Beloit to be able to travel back and forth to Milwaukee's downtown area and beyond more easily. Unaware of the city's renewal directive, residents had no chance of saving their homes because they were not properly informed of the city's plan. It was not until heavy machinery and bulldozers appeared at many of their back doors, that most residents realized what was taking place. Huge parts of the community would soon vanish from Milwaukee maps; and the dispersal of African Americans and their businesses would follow as housing shortages increased.

Walnut Street Business District 1950's
Courtesy of Milwaukee Public Library

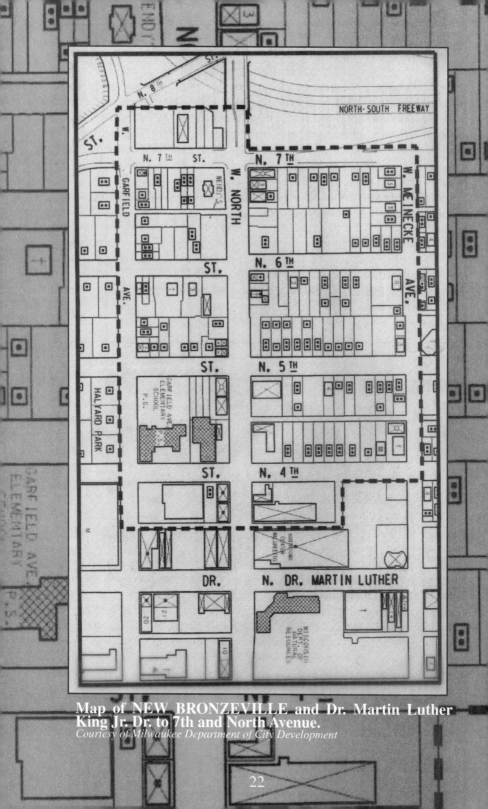

Map of NEW BRONZEVILLE and Dr. Martin Luther King Jr. Dr. to 7th and North Avenue.
Courtesy of Milwaukee Department of City Development

chapter five

Epilogue

The city of Milwaukee was then shaken by the 1968 Fair Housing marches which were supported by the NAACP Youth Council, The Commando's and Father James Groppi, a White Catholic priest. Hundreds of African Americans and Whites entered onto Milwaukee's downtown streets for 200 days of marching (17). The strength of the African American community would soon reach a new level with the U.S. Passage of Fair Housing Act, which made it illegal to discriminate in housing based on race, national origin, gender, family status, religion or handicap. The Fair Housing Act enabled African Americans to gain the substantial housing they had been searching for. Immediately, Milwaukee's African American population began to rebuild their community with the help of WACIO (Walnut Improvement Council) which built a small community on the Western boarder of the old Bronzeville community (18).

The most romanticized area however is Halyard Park, named after Wilbur and Ardie Halyard who founded Columbia Savings and Loan Association in 1925. Halyard Park was built on the Northern tip of the once thriving Bronzeville community (19). Established in 1976, Beechie Brooks, president of United Realty Group, took land that was once labeled deteriorated and transformed it into an upper middle class African American community. Each home, most in ranch style, is customized to fit the buyer's specifications (20). More than 40 African American families moved to Halyard Park. Currently, Halyard Park is getting much attention from African American families who are seeking to move back to the area.

Historical Walnut Street would receive its historical due. Mayor John O. Norquist, County Executive Tom Ament, Alderwoman Marlene Johnson Odom, along with the help of residents, have recreated Walnut Street, the hub of African American life in the 1930s and 1940s (21). This replicated Walnut Street, is located in the lower level of the Lapham Park high-rise. This replica, equipped with barbershops, a pool hall, and mock trolley tracks, offers an emotional and historical link for Lapham seniors. Truly the replica maintains the Bronzeville community atmosphere in which seniors and their families can socialize with neighbors.

23

Since the 1976 Halyard housing development, more recognition of old Bronzeville era is taking place by the City of Milwaukee to transform parts of the area along North Avenue between Historic Dr. Martin Luther King Jr. Drive and North Seventh Street, into an African American Cultural and Entertainment District. This effort has been supported by former Milwaukee Mayor John Norquist, Mayor Marvin Pratt, and now, Mayor Tom Barrett. The Martin Luther King Economic Development Corporation, Historic King Drive Business Improvement District and the Inner City Redevelopment Corporation are also supporters and stake holders of the African American Cultural and Entertainment District.

The plans of this new development have been on the minds of the community since the 1949 Urban Renewal Act. Furnished with restaurants, specialty shops, night clubs, offices, housing and open markets are the City's goal to make this area a unique place for celebrating historical African American life and culture (22). Entrepreneurs of diverse cultural backgrounds are making their way back to the area, reclaiming the spirit of the once lost, but never forgotten Bronzeville.

Much can be said about Milwaukee's diverse history, enriched with many cultures and ethnic backgrounds. The city has preserved the history of many cultures. Now Milwaukee's African American history will take its rightful place among them receiving due honor for its unique cultural contributions. Bronzeville was more than just a name and more than just a place or time. It was an African American lifestyle that could be traced all the way to West African villages. The whole community cared for all the children no matter whose child they were. The community elected their own mayors like Anthony J. Josey, who was Bronzeville's first African American mayor, housed their own doctors, teachers, and engineers. Bronzeville was a city within a city, an African American metropolis which can still be felt today in the hearts and souls of those who lived, experienced, and shared in it.

In Honor of Lower Walnut Street Businesses and the People Who Made it Happen

"As the African American community in Milwaukee continues to rebuild, it is important that homage is paid to those who came before us. Without these vital stepping stones African Americans may not have existed here. The city's youth need to be well informed about our culture and the history of African American people in Milwaukee. If not, history will repeat itself. If we allow this to happen, we as people will be lost forever."

IVORY ABENA BLACK

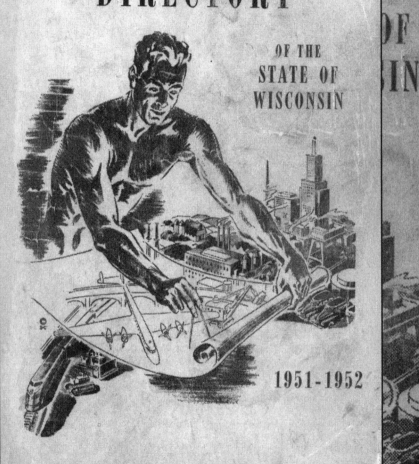

NEGRO BUSINESS DIRECTORY

OF THE STATE OF WISCONSIN

1951-1952

The Negro Business Directory of the State of Wisconsin

This directory was a guide to the businesses in Bronzeville.
A treasure chest of African American owned businesses,
organizations, doctors, lawyers and community leaders.
Courtesy of Irene Goggans and Jerrel Jones

ARTHUR CRITTENDEN

BARITONE   PIANIST

Teacher of Voice and Piano
Coaching for Recitals, Concerts, Radio, and Sacred Literature
Theory—Sight-singing—Voice Production, Breathing-Diction—Expression—Style
MUSIC STUDIO, 2022 North 6th Street—Call for Appointments—LOcust 2-6063
"LEARN TO SING WITH POISE—PLAY WITH ASSURANCE"

National Evangelistic Soloist
For Engagements Contact
J. L. Ross at 1718 West Juneau Avenue
or Call WEst 3-2665

LOUIS JABS SMOKE SHOP

Complete Line Nationally Known
Brands of Cigarettes and
Cigars and Candies

1115 West Vliet Street

BRoadway 2-9674

20th CENTURY RECREATION

2663 N. Teutonia Ave.

Open Bowling

Every
Saturday and Sunday
Afternoon and Evening
Also Holidays

COncord 4-9801

Hack's Warehouse Outlet

● Gas Ranges ● Television ● Refrigerators ● Quality Furniture ● Washers ● Heaters.

Your Credit Is Good at Hack's

333 W. Juneau Ave.   BR. 2-6530

Modern Mortgages, Inc.

745 North Plankinton Avenue
DAly 8-2661   Milwaukee 3

NEIGHBORHOOD BEVERAGE MART

Choice
Liquors — Wines
Beer — Soda

Connie and Kelly Fix, Prop.

1549 N. 12th St.

WEst 3-9324

HANOVER

3 BEARS SODA

Highest Quality

Most Popular Soda Water

DIvision 2-2500

ST. MARKS AFRICAN METHODIST EPISCOPAL CHURCH

"The Friendly Church"

MARKS AFRICAN METHODIST EPISCO

The Negro Business Directory
of the State of Wisconsin
1951-1952

"The Friendly Church"

arks the first church of its kind to be organized in the S
ed in 1869 with eight members, at a room the eight memb
ring Street, now known as Wisconsin Ave., and the buildi
Gimbels site. The first pastor was Rev. Theodore Crosby.

25, 1869 St. Marks purchased the church on the corner of
time the church was known as The First African Metho
aukee, Wisconsin. In 1883 the old church building was
il 1886 under the pastorate of Rev. W. R. Alexander tha
uilding the new structure was begun March, 1887, the ba

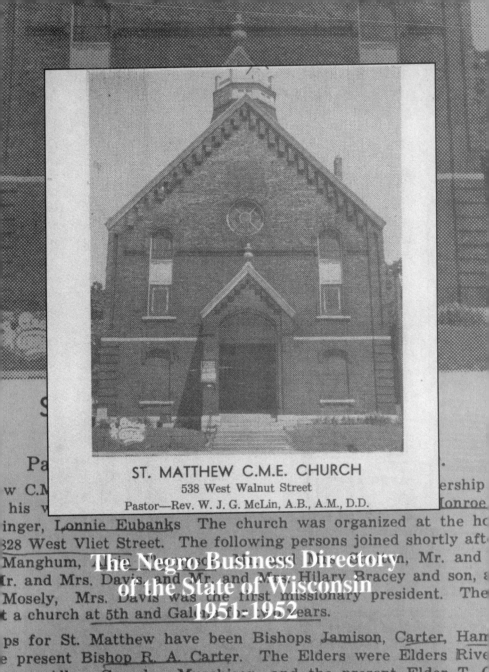

ST. MATTHEW C.M.E. CHURCH
538 West Walnut Street
Pastor—Rev. W. J. G. McLin, A.B., A.M., D.D.

S

Pa

w C.M.   ership

his v   Monroe

inger, Lonnie Eubanks The church was organized at the ho

328 West Vliet Street. The following persons joined shortly aft

Manghum,   n, Mr. and

Mr. and Mrs. Davis, and Mr. and Mrs. Hilary Bracey and son, a

Mosely, Mrs. Davis was the first missionary president. The

t a church at 5th and Gal   ears.

ps for St. Matthew have been Bishops Jamison, Carter, Ham

e present Bishop R. A. Carter. The Elders were Elders Rive

rner, Allen, Crowder, Murchison, and the present Elder T. C

ors were Rev. W. S. Ferguson, G. W. Samples, W. H. Parks, V

win, J. T. Cockran, W. H. Anderson, G. S. Smith, J. W. Ba

Coggins, and the present pastor, Rev. W. J. G. McLin.

nt church was purchased May, 1919, with the first named men

nd today is one of the leading churches in the state of Wisconsi

"A CHURCH WHERE YOU CAN FIND YOURSELF AND

NEW HOPE BAPTIST CHURCH

538 West Galena Street

BRoadway 2-0521

Rev. R. L. Lathan, Pastor

ORDER OF SERVICE

Sunday School	9:45 a. m.
Morning Service	11:00 a. m.
B. T. U.	6:30 p. m.
Evening Service	7:30 p. m.
Wednesday Evening	7:30 p. m. Prayer

REV. R. L. LATHAN

"WILL YOU PLEASE BE OUR GUEST SOON?"

"Show me the ways, O Lord; teach me thy paths.—Psalm 25, 4

REV. VIRGUS MOORE

Rev. Virgus Moore, Pastor and founder of the Evergreen Baptist Church was born in Bienville Parish, Louisiana. At the age of twelve years, he moved to McKamie, Ark. He studied ministry at the age of 21 in Stamps, Arkansas, and worked in the Evangelistic and pastoral field until 1942 when he came to Milwaukee.

Rev. Moore attended the American Baptist Theological Seminary at Nashville, Tenn.

REV. VERGUS MOORE

1859 No. 7th St.

Parsonage:
826 W. Reservoir Ave.
LOcust 2-2677

and a few members who purchased property at 1932
, and paid for this property. Rev. Crockett resigned

y at 901 W. North Ave., on which the Metropolitan

MT.

MT. ERA BAPTIST CHURCH

919 West Galena Street

REV. C. B. STOKES

Mason Temple Church of God in Christ

1932 North 9th Street

ORDER OF SERVICE

Sunday School ....10:00 A.M.
Sunday Service ....12:00 Noon
Y. P. W. W. .... 6:30 P.M.
Sunday Preaching ...... 8:30 P.M.
Tuesday Night Regular Service
Wednesday—Weekly Pastoral
Night

Parsonage—COncord 4-5043
Parsonage address—2015 North 8th
Mrs. Gladys Johnson, Church
Secretary

*"I was glad when they said unto
me, let us go into the house of the
LORD.—Psalms 122-1..*

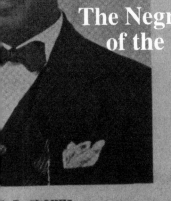

Sunday School ....10:00 A.M.
Sunday Service ....12:00 Noon
Y. P. W. W. .... 6:30 P.M.
Sunday Preaching ...... 8:30 P.M.
Tuesday Night Regular Service
Wednesday—Weekly Pastoral
Night
Parsonage—COncord 4-5043
Parsonage address—2015 North 8th
Mrs. Gladys Johnson, Church
Secretary

*"I was glad when they said unto
me, let us go into the house of the
LORD.—Psalms 122-1..*

**William V. and Cassandra Kelly
of the Milwaukee Urban League**
(circa 1945). *Courtesy of Irene Goggans*

BLACK HERITAGE

Part I

Black History Week February 11-17

SPECIAL SUPPLEMENT TO

The MILWAUKEE COURIER

SECTION III

Supplement Courtesy of Normajean Suns
Supplement published by the Milwaukee Courier February 1973
Publisher Jerrel Jones

February 17, 1973

Dear Community:

Thank You for your response to our request for information regarding the Black man's past and present in Milwaukee, Wisconsin. While seeking information on the Black man's sojourn in this city we have renewed old acquaintances and made new friends.

The joint efforts of the undersigned is only a periscopic view into the Black man's journey in Milwaukee. We sincerely called upon you, our community, for guidance and know that your input was instrumental in bringing about a meaningful supplement. Come walk with us through our past and some of our present...

Sincerely,

Fred Birts
Mary Gore
Sandra Dickerson
Josephine Hill
Pauline Teat
Evelyn Johnson

Fred Birts
Mary Gore

THE MILWAUKEE COURIER

THE NEAR NORTH SIDE BUSINESSMEN'S
ADVANCEMENT ASSOCIATION 4-3-51

THE NEAR NORTHSIDE
Businessmen's Advancement
Association at a gathering on April 3,
1951. Some of the businessmen pictured
are Harry Turner, J. Anthony Josey
(the state's first Black newspaper
publisher), "Shorty" Moore (first
Black disc jockey), Isaac Coggs, Atty.
Theodore Coggs, Larry Hill, Calvin
Moody, Emile O'Bee, French Griffin,
and Robert Starms.

APPOINTED IN 1959, the late Atty.
James Dorsey was the first Black
court commissioner in the city's
history. Atty. Dorsey is pictured with
Odell Johnson (an unsuccessful can-
didate for county supervisor in 1972),
after presenting him the Northside
YMCA Citizenship Award in 1959.

DR. GARNETT HERRON, the
first Black doctor in Milwaukee
specializing in treating diseases
of the genital-urinary tract (now
known as urology). Dr. Herron's
office was located in the downtown area and his patients mostly
white. He attended public school
in Milwaukee, as well as
Marquette university.

4

MS IRENE COGGS (fourth from right) was the discussion leader at the first young people's seminar when the Northside YMCA was on Sixth and North ave. Ralph Jefferson (standing) was youth director. Some of the

young people were Molly Jones, Nellie Parks, Betty Carter, Calvin Lewis, Walter Calvin, Geraldine Matthews, Bobby Baldwin, Rufus Crawley, Roy Kemp, Melvin Hall, and Lovetta Jones.

"MILWAUKEE'S FINEST" in the early 1960's. Policemen (seated, from left) John Crosby, Wilbon Lancaster, Aaron Hall, LeRoy Jones, and Oliver Sams. Second row (from left) Ralph Lee, Charles Benford, Calvin Moody, Al Wright, and Lonnie Spencer. Back row (from left) Felmers Chaney, Bobby Brown, Dewey Russ, Cloyce Burns, George Willis, George Johnson, Proctor Kirk, and LeRoy Harmon.

About the cover

Born of slave parents in St. Charles, Mo. Calvin Reeves came to Milwaukee in 1864 with a wounded officer of the Union army. Reeves served as a water boy for the Union forces in the Civil War.

Learning the cooper trade here, Reeves worked at that trade for several years, but horses were his real love, and he spent more than 40 years here breaking horses to harness, training them for speed, and driving them. For three years he operated a livery stable at East State and North Edison streets, providing hacks for funerals and buggies for Sunday afternoon rides.

Reeves was a member for years of the Washington Park Driving club, and for a time he trained horses at the old National park at South 22nd and West Layton streets. He once handled horses for the late August Uihlein.

He was a member of the Calvary Baptist church.

Among Reeves' survivors was Leroy J. Simmons, one of four grandchildren. Simmons was an early Black member of the state assembly.

Reeves died September 18, 1944, and the funeral was arranged by O'Bee Funeral home, located at the 1767 N. 7th st. He was buried in Union cemetery.

DR. LAURIE L. ALLEN, the first Black doctor on the staff of the Milwaukee County Hospital, from the 1920s, at Muirdale TB sanitarium. Dr. Allen also served on the board of the Milwaukee Urban League in the 1930s.

WHAT WAS LABELLED "the first social gathering of the year" around 1940. Some of the women pictured were Ms. Brawley, Ms. Carter, Ms. O'Bee, Ms. Bevenue and Ms. Rose.

WHEN VISITING MILWAUKEE celebrities used to eat at Clara's Restaurant, operated by Mr. and Ms. Harry Turner at 2417 N. 2nd st. This is a 1937 picture of the interior. Among famous people who used to stop there were Cab Calloway, Fats Waller, the Ink Spots, the Globetrotters, Duke Ellington, Bill Robinson, Louis Armstrong, Jesse Owens, Lionel Hampton, Peg Leg Bates, Willie Mays, Marvel Lewis, Josephine Baker, Adeline Hall, and the Mills Brothers.

FELMERS O. CHANEY became the first Black president of a predominantly Black-owned and managed bank when the North Milwaukee State Bank was founded on February 12, 1971. Chaney had retired from the Milwaukee police department, having served as a sergeant for a number of years.

ONE OF THE TWO first Black teachers in the Milwaukee public school system was Ms. Millie White in the early 1930s. She later married Ray Jefferson, and the couple bought a grocery store. Ms. White first taught at Fourth Street school.

5

THE 25TH WEDDING AN-
NIVERSARY of the former
pastor of St. Mark AME church,
Rev. and Ms. E. Stewart (seated,
center). Others identified at the
anniversary were the late Rev.
Issac Milton Coggs, father of the
late Atty. Ted Coggs and former
Assemblyman Isaac Coggs, Rev.
and Ms. Cecil A. Fisher, Mr. and
Ms. Sadie Thomas, and Ms.
Prosser.

MS. MILDRED SELLERS was
the first Black woman to
graduate from the old Milwaukee
Vocational School barber college.
After graduating, she served an
apprenticeship under the late
Rev. Sydney Connors in his shop
at Tenth and Walnut sts. After
working a year as a journeyman
barber and another year as a
master barber, Ms. Sellers
became the first Black woman in
Milwaukee to open her own shop
at 1118 W. Vliet st. in 1953. In 1958
she moved to 1212 W. Walnut. Ms.
Sellers's shop is presently
located at 3283 N. Green Bay ave.

JUDSON MINOR, the first
known Black policeman in
Milwaukee. Minor was sworn
into the department in October,
1924, but resigned two years
later. His beat was around city
hall and the east side. He was
assigned to the police station at
12th and W. Vine sts. Officer
Minor was not necessarily
assigned to the Black community, and his arrest powers
were not racially restricted.
Minor retired from Wehr Steel
company in the middle 1960s.

Milwaukee Heritage Guide

ONE OF THE EARLY graduating classes of the Sears Charm School, conducted by Ms. Marie Gaines (seated, center).

THE LATE REV. CECIL A. FISHER in April, 1922. Rev. Fisher was the first 'Black' probation officer in Milwaukee County. He worked for the old "Outdoor Relief" along with Dr. Fred Boho and Atty. George DeReef. Rev. Fisher was originally hired to serve Black relief recipients, but came to serve both Black and white clients.

H. B. KINNER'S RESTAURANT -featuring the "best bar-b-q in town," was located at Seventh and W. Cherry sts. In the early 1940s, Kinner was also the first Black to manufacture his own brand of sausage, which was distributed widely in stores located in the Black community.

FORMER INSURANCEMAN Theodore Mack became the first Black president of a brewery in the country when he headed a group of local businessmen who bought Peoples Brewery in Oshkosh in 1970.

KAPPA ALPHA PSI'S first ball at the UWM gym in 1943.

Milwaukee Heritage Guide

HARMONY CHAPTER, No. 107, OES, and Princess Ellah Chapter No. 22, OES. Picture was taken outside St. Mark AME church in 1939.

THE TANGENT CLUB, organized in 1922 by the student secretary of the YMCA, made an application for a branch YMCA charter in that year. Seated (from left) are Rev. Thomas, J. G. Lindsay, president; J. M. Munroe, secretary; E. Redd, and B. Holesome. Top row (from left) Ralph Blackburn, M. McMann, J. Cartwall, F. Cartwall, and C. Scott. Middle row (from left) J. E. Levy, S. H. Williams, V. Nichols, treasurer; A. Bland, C. Knox, and J. Burke.

ATTORNEY GEORGE H. DE REEF, one of the founders of the Milwaukee Urban League. Attorney De Reef is said to have trained Attorney James Dorsey.

HERBERT WARE was the owner of the first beauty salon in the state in 1963 under the national law allowing men to have their hair cut in a beauty salon. In 1970 Ware was hired by the state to teach all white instructors the technique of chemical hair straightening.

A FORMER POLICEMAN and detective, Calvin Moody was one of the first two Blacks elected to a county government office when he and Isaac Coggs were both elected county supervisors in 1964.

DANIEL RAYNOR was the first Black mortician in Milwaukee and the state. He later formed an association with his foster son, Emmitt Reed, and the funeral home was renamed Raynor and Reed. The various locations of the funeral home were Fourth and W. Cherry sts., Twelfth and W. Vliet sts., Seventh and W. Vine sts., and Sixth and W. North ave. This picture was taken in the early 1920s.

AN EARLY BLACK MARCHING band organized around 1910. The group was known as the Odd Fellows Band. Some of those pictured who later became prominent in the Milwaukee community include H. B. Klinner, Aaron Toliver, and Samuel Banks. The band would perform in all the Milwaukee County parks in Sunday afternoon concerts.

RLY BLACK MA rganized around was known as Band. Some d who later ent in the Mil nity include H. B. Toliver, and- the Milwaukee in Sunday af s.

THE URBAN LEAGUE GUILD in 1941, organized by Ms. V. Dorsey under the then MUL executive director William V. Kelly. Seated (from left) were: Ms. J. Pryor, Ms. M. Eggleston, Ms. Clardy, and Ms. C. Brown. Standing (from left) Ms. A. Jackson, Ms. J. Dorsey, Ms. M. Southhall, Ms. W. Stewart, Ms. T. Bandy, and Ms. V. Gallimore.

THEODORE HENDRICKS was the owner of a drug store at Eighth and Walnut sts. in 1930. He later moved to Seventh and Vine sts. Hendricks is pictured with his wife, who was a visiting nurse.

CARVER HI-Y CLUB. This picture was made in the attic of the "YW" cottage at 1831 N. 10th st. in 1939.

THIS IS THE FIRST group of Black women organized into a Red Cross Mothers' Club in 1941.

MONROE SWAN BECAME the first Black senator in the state when he was elected from the Sixth Senatorial District in November, 1972.

11

Milwaukee Heritage Guide

42

CARVER MEMORIAL HOMES, inc., held its first open house in December, 1944. Some of the persons pictured at the event are Frank Kirkpatrick, Larry Saunders, Ms. L. Eubanks, Ms. Bernice Lindsey, Sanford Carter, Ms. E. Jackson, and Atty. G. Hamilton.

THOMAS CHEEKS became the first Black high school teacher in the Milwaukee public school system in 1951 when he became an instructor at Lincoln high school. Cheeks also became the first Black athletic coach when he took over track and basketball at Lincoln in 1962.

MR. AND MS. C. L. JOHNSON. Johnson was the first executive director of the YMCA in the Black community. He was active with the old Booker T. Washington YMCA branch when it was first located in a home on Tenth st., and subsequently on Eighth and W. Walnut sts.

WAYNE EMBRY WAS NAMED general manager of the Milwaukee Bucks in March, 1972, making him the first Black general manager, and the highest ranking Black executive in all of the major professional sports. Embry had served as director of player personnel for the past two seasons. He originally joined the Bucks organization in the 1968-69 season as a player.

CHECKING UP AFTER the banquet for the 1967 Lincoln high school basketball champion Comets were (from left) principal A. Dunar, Andy Lewis, Frank Robinson, Sanford Carter, and athletic director Ron Foot.

16

PRESTLEY'S SCHOOL OF BEAUTY CULTURE, located at 709 W. Resevoir st., was the first Black beauty school in Wisconsin. It was owned by Ms. Mattie (Prestley) Dewese, who taught along with her foster daughter, Ms.Flora Simms. Many of Milwaukee's favorite and most popular beauticians graduated from this school, and are pictured in this early graduating class.

A TEA FOR ALL the graduating young ladies in 1952 met at the home of Ms. C. Harris. Pictured are Barbara Cabell, Joan Turner, and hostess Margarette Bobo.

CORNELIUS L. GOLIGHTLY became the first Black member of the Milwaukee school board when he was elected in April, 1961. He was subsequently appointed to the unexpired term of a resigned school board member May 2, 1961. He served until June, 1967, when he was defeated for re-election. The first and only Black school board president, Atty. Harold B. Jackson, was appointed to the board by the board in April, 1970. Jackson was elected president of the school board in July, 1971, and re-elected in July, 1972. He resigned from the board and as president in November, 1972.

ALPHA PHI ALPHA FRATERNITY was the first Black fraternity organized in Milwaukee and Wisconsin. All students at one time or other at Marquette university, pictured are Alden McDonald, Dr. Fred Bobo, Frank King Beck, Carl Bloom, B. K. Bruce Harrison (deceased), Dr. V. Nichols, J. Harvay Kams (early executive secretary of the Urban League), La Jaux Stanton, Dr. George Daniels, Dr. George Duma (from Capetown, South Africa); Rollin McMahon (deceased), and Dr. Paul K. Campbell.

LIGHTL . memb ool boa in Apr ently a d term d memb until Jun 1967, when he was defeated f re-election. The first and on Black school board presiden Atty. Harold B. Jackson, wa appointed to the board by th board in April, 1970. Jackson wa elected president of the scho board in July, 1971, and r elected in July, 1972. He resigne from the board and as presiden in November, 1972.

SUPERVISOR CLINTON ROSE as he appeared in a picture taken in Boston, Mass., in 1937. Rose was the first Black person elected to the County Board of Supervisors to partially represent a suburban area. He was first elected in 1970.

THE NEW LAPHAM PARK swimming pool was the location of the first swimming meet held in the Black community back in the early 1940s. Participants in the meet included (from left) Willie Harold, Lincoln Gaines, Andrew Lewis, Jackie Love (deceased), and Pat Goggins.

PRINCESS ELLA CHAPTER No. 1, OES, Ester Day in June, 1922. Ladies identified are Ms. Roach, Weaver, Sanford, Morley, Ward, Perkins, Miles, Wilson, Owens, Baylor, Raynor, Grace, and Lewis.

PROBABLY THE HOLDER of more Blacks "firsts" than any other Black person in Wisconsin is Atty. Vel R. Phillips. Her most recent, and possibly most notable, "first" was becoming the state's first Black judge when she was sworn into office as Childrens Court Judge in August, 1971. She had been appointed by Governor Patrick Lucey, but lost a bid for re-election. Prior to the appointment, Atty. Phillips had served more than 15 years as an alderman. She was the first Black on the Common Council, having been elected for the first time in 1956. In 1958 Atty. Phillips became the first Black person named to a national committee of either major political party. She was named Wisconsin national committeewoman for the Democratic party. Atty. Phillips was also the first Black woman to receive a degree from the University of Wisconsin Law School, when she was awarded the degree from the University of Wisconsin Law School. In 1961, in the same year, with her husband, Dale, they became the first (Black or white) man and wife law team to be admitted to practice law in Wisconsin.

DR. GEORGE W. LANE (standing third from right) was named director of the Sickle Cell Center at Deaconess Hospital last year. He is pictured with members of his family. Seated (from left) are Ms. Laura Lane, Alfonso Sanders (brother-in-law), Ms. Lula Lane (mother), and Ms. Mildred Sanders (sister). Standing (from left) are Ms. Willie Jefferson (sister), Ralph Jefferson (brother-in-law), Ms. Bertha Ward (sister), Dr. Lane, Ms. Mary Pryor, (sister), and Joe Pryor (brother-in-law).

Milwaukee Heritage Guide

THE HOLDER of more Blacks "firsts" than any other Black person in Wisconsin is Atty. Vel R. Phillips. Her most recent, and possibly most notable, "first" was becoming the state's first Black judge when she was sworn into office as Childrens Court Judge in August, 1971. She had been appointed by Governor Patrick Lucey, but lost a bid for re-election. Prior to the appointment, Atty. Phillips had served more than 15 years as an alderman. She was the first Black on the Common Council, elected for the first time in 1958. Atty. Phillips became the first Black person named to a national committee of either major political party. She was named Wisconsin national committeewoman for the Democratic party. Atty. Phillips was also the first Black woman to receive a degree from the University of Wisconsin Law School, when she was awarded the degree from the University of Wisconsin Law School, in 1961. In the same year, with her husband, Dale, they became the first (Black or white) man and wife law team to be admitted to practice law in Wisconsin.

DR. GEORGE W. LANE (standing third from right) was named director of the Sickle Cell Center at Deaconess Hospital last year. He is pictured with members of his family. Seated

in November, 1943, as this picture will attest. Some of the hunters pictured are Allex Bassett, Walter Hampton, and "Dewey."

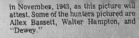

THE MILWAUKEE COURIER

IT WAS A SUCCESSFUL deer hunting season for the Rod and Gun Club back in November, 1943, as this picture will attest. Some of the hunters pictured are Allex Bassett, Walter Hampton, and "Dewey."

"SADIE HAWKINS" Day with a teen club at the Northside YMCA. Pictured are (from right) Donald Goggans, Evelyn Bailey, Floyd Campbell, Marcia Hall, and Dorothy Bailey.

MS. CAROLE (THOMAS) MALONE was the recipient of the Northside YMCA Citizenship Award in 1954. Donor, and maker of the presentation was Wilbur Halyard, founder of Columbia Savings and Loan Association, the first Black financial institution in the state.

AN EARLY CHURCH CHOIR of St. Mark AME church located in the early 1920s on Fourth and W. Galena sts. Some of the choir members who can be identified include Consuella Wilson, Bert Revels and daughter, and Daniel Raynor.

19

BOOKER T. WASHINGTON Y.M.C.A.
1946 CAMPING GROUP

FIRST GROUP OF BLACK youngsters who went to the YMCA Camp Minikani in 1946. Andrew Lewis (standing at left) was the leader. Some of the youngsters pictured are Leroy Ware, Mickey Tabor, Buzzy Wilson, Douglas Jones, Vernon Ware, Freddy Jones, Warner Birts, Jerrel Jones, Jack Wilson, William Fisher, Roscoe Webb, Fred Birts, and Kermit Hood.

DR. LOUIS T. MAXEY became the first Black president and board chairman of a hospital in Wisconsin when the Wisconsin Hospital & Geriatric Treatment Center opened in August, 1971.

WILLIAM V. KELLY, executive director of the Milwaukee Urban League, was honored on April 13, 1950, for his 21 years on the job. Presenting Kelly with a life membership in the YMCA and a briefcase were Sidney Sayles (left) and Lincoln Gaines. Kelly was the MUL's first executive director, having held the post since 1929.

Milwaukee Heritage Guide

REV. M. J. BATTLE was named the YMCA "Man of the Year" in 1955. He served as pastor of Calvary Baptist church for many years.

L'ALLEGRO CLUB, a social club of the old Booker T. Washington YMCA. Identified in this 1946 pictured of the club are Bernadine Jefferson, Dorothy Fisher, Wilma Jefferson, Lillian Brown, Buster Gallimore, Irene Goggins, Arthur Bacon, and Collie Carter.

GALILEE BAPTIST CHURCH youth groups in 1946. Members of the "Five Notes" were Freddie Royal, Jimmy Whitfield, Robert Lott, and two unidentified youth. The "Estralaita" members were Romelia Hamm Powell, Juaniti Hamm Virgil, Maude Neal Toney, and Devella Norton Tucker.

OFFICERS OF THE Princess Ella Chapter No. 1, OES, in 1954. Some of them identified are Ms. M. Gaines, Sanford Carter, and Ms. F. Simms.

21

THE DELPHIANS Social Club in the early 1940s. Some of the members pictured are Thelma Welch, Mattiebelle Woods, Marie Gaines, Una Colin, Loretta Whyte, Arnell Rose, Ruby Kinner, Dorothy Quantrelle, and Fosteria Jones.

JACK PATTERSON in 1946 became the first Black man hired by the Milwaukee Electric Rail and Transport company. Working out of the National avenue station, Patterson operated street cars and the trackless trolley.

...YMCA at 12th
...ated back in
...at time in-
...associate
...es, physical
...nt, assistant
...Toutenhouf,
...tor; Robert
..., and Robert

THE MT. ZION BAPTIST church usher board held their anniversary in July, 1953. Reb. Lovelace, pastor, is at left, and Rev. McNeal is at right.

THE FIRST INDIAN GUIDE induction ceremony was held the old Booker T. Washington YMCA in 1946. All youth were required to bring their parents for the occasion.

E FI
ck Y
he 18
mber
eader
ded
ferso
r Ba
l The

THE DEDICATION CEREMONY of the Northside YMCA when it first moved to the location at Sixth st. and North ave. was held in September, 1950.

22

Chapter 1

1, 2, 3, 4: Caroline Quarrels, Joshua Glover, the Underground Railroads of Wisconsin, please visit:" The Milton House Historical" Site Web site,http://www.miltonhouse.org/ugrrinwi.html. Also "Freedom Train North: Stories of the Underground Railroad in Wisconsin" by Julia Pferdehirt, for a collection of true stories from people, places, and events on Wisconsin's Underground Railroad.
5: "African American Founding Fathers of Wisconsin" please contact: Heritage Wisconsin 1-800-432-8747 or http://tourism.state.wi.us 6:"Negro Recognition In Early Milwaukee", by Chester V. Salomon, collective series from the Wisconsin Black Historical Society 6:"Watson Family History" assembled by the Milwaukee Public Library, Milwaukee, Wisconsin 1994 7, 8, "The Rise of Milwaukee's Black Population", Joe William Trotter Jr., "Black Milwaukee: The Making of an Industrial Proletariat 1915-45", Illinois Books Edition 1988. Copyright 1985 by the Board of Trustees of the University of Illinois Manufactured in The United States of America "The Making of Milwaukee", John Gurda, copyright 1999 Milwaukee County Society 910 N Old World Third Street Milwaukee, WI 53202. Printed in the United States of American Burton & Mayer, Inc.

Chapter 2

9: "Blacks in Milwaukee's Labor Force", By Thomas R. Buchana, selected document from Wisconsin Black Historical Society. 10: Personal interview with Reuben Harpole, Milwaukee, Wisconsin, Subject:" Growing up in Bronzeville". Fall of 2003 by cultural anthropologist Ivory Abena Black. 11, 12: Personal interview with Reuben Harpole, Milwaukee, Wisconsin, Subject: "Mr. and Mrs. Halyard". Conducted fall of 2003 by cultural anthropologist Ivory Abena Black. Mother and Father of the African American Community. Personal interview with Reuben Harpole, Milwaukee, Wisconsin, Subject: "C.L Johnson and Bernice Copeland-Lindsay", The University Wisconsin-Milwaukee Research Profile Division, Vol19, Number 2. Or Reuben Harpole titled "Our Historian" by the Black community.

Chapter 3

13: Personal interview with Reuben Harpole Milwaukee, Wisconsin, Subject: Lower Walnut Street. Conducted fall of 2003. Personal Interview with Attorney Leonard V. Brady, Milwaukee, Wisconsin, Subject: Lower Walnut Street businesses. Conducted winter of 2003. Personal interview with Normajean Sims, Subject: Lower Walnut Street. Conducted spring of 2004 by cultural anthropologist Ivory Abena Black.

Chapter 4

14, 15: "Urban Renewal, I- 43, Streets of Bronzeville", University Archives and Records Center University of Pennsylvania," Come to Where the Knowledge Is": A History of the University City Science Center, by Mackenzie S. Carlson .Friday 3, September 1999 16: Personal interview with Reuben Harpole, Milwaukee, Wisconsin, Subject:" Growing up in Bronzeville." Conducted fall of 2003 by cultural anthropologist Ivory Abena Black.

Chapter 5

17: "Black and white and gray after 35 years, Fair Housing Act's success isn't clear-cut" By Michele Derus, Journal Sentinel, April 25, 2003 18:"Core Area Improvement Group Gets Sites for 2 Model Homes", By David M. Skoloda of the Journal Staff, Journal,March, 3, 1968. 19: "African American and the Culture of Contributions", Urban Anthropology Inc. Executive Director Jill Florence Lackey PHD.www.urban_anthropology.org. 20, 21, and 22:"Mayor Norquist, Public Officials open recreated Walnut Street at Lapham Park New Facility to Provide Emotional & Historical Link to Senior Housing Development" by John Bratina, September 25, 2000. Personal interview with Beechie Brooks, Milwaukee,Wisconsin, Subject: "Halyard Park and United Realty Group." Conducted summer of 2004 by cultural anthropologist Ivory Abena Black. Milwaukee's Bronzeville Revitalization; An African American Cultural & Entertainment District Guild, The Department of City Development-Milwaukee, Wisconsin.

Ivory Abena Black is a cultural anthropologist residing in Milwaukee and has a degree in Anthropology from the University of Wisconsin-Milwaukee. Ms. Black has tackled environmental issues at the grass roots level and cultural traditions abroad in Ghana and West Africa, she has toured Europe performing with, "A Call for Peace." She has conducted cultural walking tours with Urban Anthropology, focusing on the History of African Americans in Milwaukee. She is the International Organizer for the Ethiopian World Federation Incorporated. She is a writer and researcher for The Milwaukee Courier Newspaper. Ms. Black has taught applied anthropology courses at Marquette University. A researcher and a co-producer of "Punching In" a documentary.

Faithe Colas is publisher of the Milwaukee Courier newspaper. The Milwaukee Courier is Milwaukee's oldest African American newspaper and Wisconsin's award winning news source for the African American community. Colas is the third publisher in the history of the 40 plus year old newspaper. Colas is vice president of print for Wisconsin Black Media Association, a member of the National Association of Black Journalist, a member of the Milwaukee Press Club and a member of the Milwaukee NAACP Branch executive committee. Faithe has one daughter, Paige.

Patricia A. Diggs is a communication specialist with 25 years experience in television, radio, print publication and public relations. In Los Angeles, Ms. Diggs gained her experience at KCOP-TV, KFAC-Classical Radio, KFWB-News Radio and Group W. Cable. In Washington D.C. she was an advertising manager for the Greater Washington Society of Associated Executives and a Senior Marketing Executive at Tucker McKenzie, a public relations firm. She has traveled on assignment to England, France, Spain and Italy. Ms. Diggs attended the University Wisconsin-Milwaukee and continued her professional development in communications at the University California Los Angeles. A member of the National Association of Black Journalist and a native of Milwaukee.

Notes

Notes

Notes

Booker T. Washington Branch YMCA 7th Annual Dinner November 11, 1945
Courtesy of Irene Goggans

Y Rod & Gun Club at Booker T. Washington YMCA on 8TH and Walnut Street February 13, 1966
Courtesy of Irene Goggans

IN HONOR OF LOWER WALNUT STREET BUSINESSES AND PEOPLE WHO MADE BRONZEVILLE HAPPEN.

Green Bay Fish Market-Polansky
Bach's Deli
Brookstaff Economy Store-Rachall
818 W. Walnut St.
Tompkins Ice Cream Parlor:
Johnnie V. Caldwell
816 W. Walnut St.
Silverstein Grocery Store
Mason, N.A. Tailor Shop
732 W Walnut St.
West Indian Herb Products Co:
Rev. Chief J. Ruffino
916 W. Walnut St.
Regal Theatre: Sid Market
704 W. Walnut St.
Hillside V&V Market
Hillside Home Appliance Merchandise
612 W. Walnut St.
W.A Mason Co. Tailor Shop
732 W. Walnut St.
Matherson's Haberdashery
623 W. Walnut St.
Handsome Barber Shop: R.C Moore
828 W. Walnut St.
Reasby's Garage & Body Shop
328 W. Walnut St.
Apex Amusements-Livery Service (Cabs)
819 W. Walnut St.
Advertising (Radio): Mannie Mauldin Jr.
612 W. Walnut St.
Harlem Record & Appliance Shop
919 W. Walnut St.
NAACP: W. Dale Phillips (president)
702 A.W. Walnut St.
Attorney's: Coggs, Theodore
635 A. W. Walnut St.
Dorsey, James W.
635 W. Walnut St
Phillips, Dale
707 A.W. Walnut St.
Phillips, Mrs. Vel
707 A. W. Walnut St.
Blaskovics Inc- Live & Dresses Poultry
1101 W. Walnut St.
Colonial Barber Shop
610 W. Walnut St.
Deluxe Barber Shop
939 W. Walnut St.
Veterans Barber Shop
1017 W. Walnut St.
Blanche's Beauty Chest
726 W. Walnut St.
Deluxe Beauty Clinic
838 W. Walnut St.
Sally's Beauty Shop
1116 W. Walnut St.
Vogue Beauty Salon
923 W. Walnut St.
Josey J. Anthony-Bookkeeper
729 W. Walnut St
Carpenters & Contractors: Barron, James
907 W. Walnut St.
Robert Finney
606 W. Walnut St.
Decon Jones Chicken Shack
537 W Walnut St.
Larry's Chicken Shack
619 W. Walnut St.
Lloyd's Drug Store
725 W. Walnut St.
Boatner's Chili
709 W. Walnut St.
Dr. Kenneth L. McIver
1202 W. Walnut St.
Greater Galilee Baptist Church:
Rev. M.J. Battle (pastor)
808 W. Walnut St.
St. Matthew C.M.E. Church:
Rev. W.J.G. McLin (pastor)
Band Box Cleaners
839 W. Walnut St.

Tal & Griff's Valet Services
909 W. Walnut St.
Rev. G.W. McDuffy
710 B. W. Walnut St.
Rev. Chief J. Ruffino
916 W. Walnut St.
Rev. William Rush
508 W. Walnut St.
Rev. Maridy L. Andrews
Sidney's Furniture
1129 W. Walnut St.
Fort Nite Club: Mrs. Frank McIntyre
905 W. Walnut St.
Bentley's Clothing & Jewelry
1138 W. Walnut St.
Tastee Freez
717 W. Walnut St.
700 Tap: Bob Brown
700 W. Walnut St.
711 Taverns : Jo Harris & Willie Morris
711 W. Walnut St.
Kokomos: Bonnie Qualls
Cleo's Flowers
535 W. Walnut St.
Pembroke Coal & Ice Co.
612 W. Walnut St.
O'Bee Funeral Home: Emile O'Bee Sr.
617 W. Walnut St.
Jones Service Station
603 W. Walnut St.
Tanker Gas Station
735 W. Walnut St.
Josey J. Anthony- Income Tax Consultant
729 W. Walnut St.
Insurance Salesman Underwriter:
Leroy Simmons
1204 W. Walnut St.
Mrs. Cleo Reed- Insurance Salesman
535 W. Walnut St.
T. Joe's Self Service Launderette:
T. Joe & Ruth Thomas
718 W. Walnut St.
King Solomon-Lodge of Ancient York Mason:
Walter Taylor (grand master)
811 W. Walnut St.
James C. Jackson- 20th Century Cleaners &
Dryers Inc
332 W. Walnut St.
Mrs. Hivell Gibbs c/o Lloyd's Drugstore
(pharmacists)
725 W. Walnut St.
Physicians: Dr. Henry A. Fletcher
720 W. Walnut St.
Dr. William R. Rose
833 W. Walnut St.
Dr. Cyril F. Turney
508 W. Walnut St.
Pastine Poole Hall
1035 W. Walnut St.
725 Pool Hall
725 W Walnut St.
Johnson Agency Real Estate Agencies
921 W. Walnut St.
Clara's Restaurant
722 W. Walnut St.
Jon & Luo's Steak House
835 W. Walnut St.
Knox Music Café
608 W. Walnut St.
Lousisiana Fine Food
322 W. Walnut St.
Gold Coast Bar
638 W. Walnut St.
Riley Cook Upholstering
635 W. Walnut St.
Dr. A. R. Wiener (dentist)
Big Milt Super Bar: Milton Brill
1039 W. Walnut St.
The Bop Shop: Shorty Moore
612 W. Walnut St.

Submitted by Normajean C. Sims (BillieJo)
Historian of the Walnut Street Social Gathering

IN HONOR OF LOWER WALNUT STREET BUSINESSES
AND PEOPLE WHO MADE BRONZEVILLE HAPPEN.

Green Bay Fish Market-Polansky
Bach's Deli
Brookstaff Economy Store-Rachall
818 W. Walnut St.
Tompkins Ice Cream Parlor:
Johnnie V. Caldwell
816 W. Walnut St.
Silverstein Grocery Store
Mason, N.A. Tailor Shop
732 W Walnut St.
West Indian Herb Products Co:
Rev. Chief J. Ruffino
916 W. Walnut St.
Regal Theatre: Sid Market
704 W. Walnut St.
Hillside V&V Market
Hillside Home Appliance Merchandise
612 W. Walnut St.
W.A Mason Co. Tailor Shop
732 W. Walnut St.
Matherson's Haberdashery
623 W. Walnut St.
Handsome Barber Shop: R.C Moore
828 W. Walnut St.
Reasby's Garage & Body Shop
328 W. Walnut St.
Apex Amusements-Livery Service (Cabs)
819 W. Walnut St.
Advertising (Radio): Mannie Mauldin Jr.
612 W. Walnut St.
Harlem Record & Appliance Shop
919 W. Walnut St.
NAACP: W. Dale Phillips (president)
702 A.W. Walnut St.
Attorney's: Coggs, Theodore
635 A. W. Walnut St.
Dorsey, James W.
635 W. Walnut St
Phillips, Dale
707 A.W. Walnut St.
Phillips, Mrs. Vel
707 A. W. Walnut St.
Blaskovics Inc- Live & Dresses Poultry
1101 W. Walnut St.
Colonial Barber Shop
610 W. Walnut St.
Deluxe Barber Shop
939 W. Walnut St.
Veterans Barber Shop
1017 W. Walnut St.
Blanche's Beauty Chest
726 W. Walnut St.
Deluxe Beauty Clinic
838 W. Walnut St.
Sally's Beauty Shop
1116 W. Walnut St.
Vogue Beauty Salon
923 W. Walnut St.
Josey J. Anthony-Bookkeeper
729 W. Walnut St
Carpenters & Contractors: Barron, James
907 W. Walnut St
Robert Finney
606 W. Walnut St.
Decon Jones Chicken Shack
537 W Walnut St.
Larry's Chicken Shack
619 W. Walnut St.
Lloyd's Drug Store
725 W. Walnut St.
Boatner's Chili
709 W. Walnut St.
Dr. Kenneth L. McIver
1202 W. Walnut St.
Greater Galilee Baptist Church:
Rev. M.J. Battle (pastor)
808 W. Walnut St.
St. Matthew C.M.E. Church:
Rev. W.J.G. McLin (pastor)
Band Box Cleaners
839 W. Walnut St.

Tal & Griff's Valet Services
909 W. Walnut St.
Rev. G.W. McDuffy
710 B. W. Walnut St.
Rev, Chief J. Ruffino
916 W. Walnut St.
Rev. William Rush
508 W. Walnut St.
Rev. Maridy L. Andrews
Sidney's Furniture
1129 W. Walnut St.
Fort Nite Club: Mrs. Frank McIntyre
905 W. Walnut St.
Bentley's Clothing & Jewelry
1138 W. Walnut St.
Tastee Freez
717 W. Walnut St.
700 Tap: Bob Brown
700 W. Walnut St.
711 Taverns : Jo Harris & Willie Morris
711 W. Walnut St.
Kokomos: Bonnie Qualls
Cleo's Flowers
535 W. Walnut St.
Pembroke Coal & Ice Co.
612 W. Walnut St.
O'Bee Funeral Home: Emile O'Bee Sr.
617 W. Walnut St.
Jones Service Station
603 W. Walnut St.
Tanker Gas Station
735 W. Walnut St.
Josey J. Anthony- Income Tax Consultant
729 W. Walnut St.
Insurance Salesman Underwriter:
Leroy Simmons
1204 W. Walnut St.
Mrs. Cleo Reed- Insurance Salesman
535 W. Walnut St.
T. Joe's Self Service Launderette:
T. Joe & Ruth Thomas
718 W. Walnut St.
King Solomon-Lodge of Ancient York Mason:
Walter Taylor (grand master)
811 W. Walnut St.
James C. Jackson- 20th Century Cleaners &
Dryers Inc
332 W. Walnut St.
Mrs. Hivell Gibbs c/o Lloyd's Drugstore
(pharmacists)
725 W. Walnut St.
Physicians: Dr. Henry A. Fletcher
720 W. Walnut St.
Dr. William R. Rose
833 W. Walnut St.
Dr. Cyril F. Turney
508 W. Walnut St.
Pastine Poole Hall
1035 W. Walnut St.
725 Pool Hall
725 W Walnut St.
Johnson Agency Real Estate Agencies
921 W. Walnut St.
Clara's Restaurant
722 W. Walnut St.
Jon & Luo's Steak House
835 W. Walnut St.
Knox Music Café
608 W. Walnut St.
Lousiana Fine Food
322 W. Walnut St.
Gold Coast Bar
638 W. Walnut St.
Riley Cook Upholstering
635 W. Walnut St.
Dr. A. R. Wiener (dentist)
Big Milt Super Bar: Milton Brill
1039 W. Walnut St.
The Bop Shop: Shorty Moore
612 W. Walnut St.

Submitted by Normajean C. Sims (BillieJo)
Historian of the Walnut Street Social Gathering

Bronzeville - A Milwaukee Lifestyle

C. L. and Cleopatra Johnson in Ideal Tailors 1930's
Courtesy of Irene Goggans

Walnut Street Business District 1950's
Courtesy of Milwaukee Public Library

Courtesy of Irene Goggans